The Prestige

East Midland

John Banks

Photography by G H F Atkins

ISBN 1 898432 42 2

A note about vehicle identification -- Vehicles were sometimes renumbered during their life in the East Midland fleet, although this happened much less with this operator than with some others. The convention in this book is to **embolden** the vehicle's identity at the date of the photograph.

Front Cover Illustration -- A reappearance of the older livery came in fine style on this ex-London Transport Routemaster. The former RM1164 (164CLT) had been reregistered **NSG636A** in this August 1990 view at Mansfield.

Title Page Illustration -- The prewar face of East Midland is epitomised by Leyland Tiger **B10** (**BAL610**) at Huntingdon Street, Nottingham in August 1935. This type of Brush body was more often encountered, with other operators, with a front-entrance; in its early years East Midland was firmly wedded to the rear entrance.

Rear Cover Illustration -- An earlier recreation of East Midland's yellow, cream and brown livery was applied to a 1965 Leyland Atlantean **178** (**DNN178C**) for the Company's fiftieth anniversary in 1977. This scene was in Chesterfield in June 1977.

Rear Cover Insets --Like many other companies, East Midland specified radiator badges cast in the Company's name rather than the manufacturer's. These examples are from 1935's Leyland TS7 Tiger **B11** (**BAL611**) and TD4 Titan **D6** (**BAL706**).

Produced for the Publishers
Venture Publications, Glossop, Derbyshire
by John Banks, Romiley, Cheshire
using computerised origination

THE PHOTOGRAPHER

Railway photographers seem to be a more celebrated race than are their road transport brethren. And there were quite different sorts of output from the great names: Henry Casserley simply tried to photograph every steam locomotive in existence, for example; Ernest Wethersett was the master at placing a train and its locomotive in the classic topographical settings of the southern part of the LNER; Wethersett's protégé, Bishop Eric Treacy, produced a technically superb photograph for its own sake; such lesser luminaries as Arthur Cawston and Arthur Mace - clergymen both - attacked a wide range of subjects and settings with equal facility and felicity; and so on. Of the road vehicle photographers in the pre-war period, the name of Bill Brunell stands out. But he photographed motorcars. First-class bus photographers from the early days can be counted on one's fingers. Perhaps the best of them was, and is, Geoffrey Atkins who, at the age of 87 and having taken his first bus photograph in 1927, still occasionally takes a camera with him on walks in his home town of Nottingham.

Geoffrey Atkins was, first and foremost, also a railway photographer. His technique surely influenced his better known bus photography. He may never have known Bill Brunell's work with the motorcar, but one cannot help feeling that he may have seen it in contemporary periodicals and been influenced by it, too, for across eight decades he has done for the bus and coach what Brunell did for the private car; what, indeed, Treacy did for the railway train.

When discussing with Geoffrey the content of the first *"Prestige Series"* album of his photographs, United Automobile Services Ltd was chosen. United gave birth to East Midland Motor Services Ltd, which was Geoffrey's favourite local company operator. East Midland selected itself, then, as Number Two in the series.

Geoffrey Atkins has lived in Nottingham all his life. Mansfield, Chesterfield and Doncaster are not far away and were frequently visited, cameras at the ready. Early East Midland views were of buses of the G- and M-classes that were a direct link with United. From 1930 onwards there is a practically unbroken line of sparkling pictures of East Midland standard types, usually taken when they were still new and in original condition.

*One of the 1927 G-types, **G8** (**RR7408**), at Westgate, Mansfield in November 1934.*

It has to be stressed that Geoffrey Atkins had his own methods when photographing, much as did the railway photographers mentioned above. In his case the aim was to provide a visual record of coachwork on public service vehicles. Back in the good old days of sharp distinctions between municipal, company and independent operators, all of whom were able to call upon the services of a host of coachbuilders now no more, bus fleets in Great Britain had a clearly defined character, a situation which lasted more or less to the end of 1968 and the coming of the National Bus Company. Municipality, BET, Tilling, large independent, small independent... They all had their favourite coachbuilder. Sometimes the unthinkable happened, and an allegiance was changed. Sometimes operators favoured more than one provider of bodywork as a matter of policy (today that would be called "dual-sourcing", then it was known as "not putting all your eggs in one basket"). Often, a voluble salesman caused such a change. For all or any of those reasons there was, albeit within a fairly stable environment, much variety.

Geoffrey Atkins has comprehensively recorded many of the larger operators, from London Transport in the South to United in the North. He is not a registration-number collector. Not for him the striving to find that last one of a batch of ten, twenty, or fifty, standard Guy Arab utilities, Eastern Coach Works Bristols or Weymann AEC Regents. And how relaxing that must have been in his heyday. To paraphrase Oscar Wilde, there is only one thing worse than seeking out that last missing registration number, and that is finding it. The Atkins technique has been to produce an image of the coachbuilder's art. If only one angle was recorded, one can be sure that it shows the product to best advantage. Often, two or more were put on film, and then it didn't matter that they might be of the same bus. Its identity was secondary to the chance of the right shot of the body. The location, too, was incidental to the main object. If a place was good for photography (Huntingdon Street springs to mind), it was used time and time again.

Some might consider this method disadvantageous. Nor, perhaps, would the comparative paucity of Geoffrey Atkins's coverage of the smaller independents strike the completist sympathetically; a lack which also led to vehicles taken over from small operators receiving less attention than standard types forming part of the design and development chain followed by municipal and company operators in collaboration with the coachbuilding industry. The present writer, for example, when browsing through the matchless Atkins pre-war London Transport collection, was surprised at the absence of former independents' buses. "They didn't interest me," was the disarming reply when I asked why he had never photographed any of the first London Transport TD-class of acquired Leyland Titans.

This is as it should be. Wethersett could not have done Casserley's work, nor Cawston Treacy's. The writer often photographs motorcars, among other subjects, but could not hope to be another Bill Brunell. Just so is Geoffrey Atkins's work unique. One look at a GHFA print, especially if it comes from his own enlarger, and there can be no doubt in the viewer's mind. "That's an Atkins," he will murmur and not complain about the gaps. What we have is a remarkable visual catalogue of over sixty years of bodywork development from, in this case, one of the most characterful operators of them all.

Geoffrey Atkins has never been profligate in his use of film. It would be foreign to him to run round a bus station photographing everything in sight. Thus over more than sixty years he has amassed between eight and nine hundred East Midland negatives: an average of fifteen per year. Each shot has been carefully chosen and had to be exactly what was wanted. He is by no means a fair-weather photographer, though. Shots in pouring rain, snow, and even fog, can be found among his masterpieces. He is a peerless producer of night shots, too, and not only in the relatively calm surroundings of a bus station. Above all, he has never stinted on

"A peerless producer of night shots." Huntingdon Street, Nottingham in January 1937.

equipment. His cameras, lenses and enlarging equipment are carefully chosen to produce the results he personally wants. And that is what his collection is: personal. The pictures have never been taken with publication in mind and a great many of them never have been published. This album can contain little more than ten percent of the GHFA East Midland work. The choice has naturally fallen on what might be termed "the golden years", which can be taken to mean up to and including the first generation of rear-engined double-deckers. Most of the pre-war subjects chose themselves, as did what coverage Geoffrey wanted at the time of acquired operators' vehicles, especially those from Baker Brothers.

As with the previous book in this series, I am grateful to Philip Battersby and Ron Maybray for help so unstintingly given: without their generous assistance, indeed, the book might still have appeared but would have been the poorer for its lack. I also acknowledge with thanks the help with early company ephemera kindly given by Mr P Cartwright of East Midland Motor Services Ltd. The PSV Circle two-volume fleet history of the Company has been particularly useful in ensuring that the GHFA photographs in the main body of this book are presented in - broadly - chronological order. Principal thanks go, as before, to Mr Geoffrey Atkins. His patience in the face of the writer's ceaseless questions, his help in selecting the photographs, his invaluable reminiscences and, above all, his encyclopaedic knowledge of coachwork have made this album and its fellows worthy additions to our shelves. In particular, he has provided all dates and locations quoted in the captions. "I am glad that some of these photographs will reach a wider audience," was his comment after we had chosen the East Midland views. So are we.

East Midland kept alive the pre-1930 United livery for twenty-six years after United suppressed it.

THE COMPANY

East Midland… Every operator will have its own aura for each reader. Some are simply unknown. Some are mysterious: the China Bus Company can and does interest. It is exotic enough to catch the imagination of the enthusiast who has never been further south-east than Canvey Island. Massive picture collections are built up and pored over of such subjects as Glasgow trams or Samuel Ledgard buses by enthusiasts who never saw one; who may, indeed, have been as yet unborn when such things disappeared from the streets. But we all have our local favourites, plus one or two that became almost as well-known through visiting relations in foreign parts or going on holiday to distant areas of the country, or even out of it.

The writer was brought up among the dizzying blue and white swoops and whirls of Kingston-upon-Hull Corporation's Guy Arabs and AEC Regents, and the weird, domed-roof fleet of East Yorkshire Motor Services Ltd. That combination was a hard act to follow; they were two of the most characterful fleets in the country. With grandparents and various of his uncles, aunts and cousins living in the Nottinghamshire/Derbyshire border regions, however, he found that East Midland could quite hold its own with the hometown product. The only memory of riding on wooden slatted seats upstairs in a wartime Guy Arab is a gift of East Midland. One of the uncles was a forester in Clumber Park, part of Sherwood Forest. Several exciting holidays were spent in the tiny Clumber Park village of Hardwick in the nineteen-fifties. To say that, in an era when car ownership was still a dream for most people, we were isolated and forgotten by the world would not be so far from the truth. The postman came, of course, as did a mobile shop. And so did East Midland: twice a week, on Wednesday and Saturday market days, to take us into Worksop. The bus was always a single-decker, and memory supplies a picture of an AEC radiator and those beautifully flared side-panels. And the livery…

That yellow, cream and brown was a direct link with United Automobile Services Ltd, from which East Midland had sprung, fully formed, in 1927. The genesis lay with W T Underwood at Clowne, who began operations in the Autumn of 1920, connecting Clowne with Worksop, Bolsover and Mansfield, and who expanded rapidly in the area, acquiring competitors as early as 1922. Underwood had behind him the considerable weight of E B Hutchinson of United, a situation that was not long hidden from Underwood's competitors. With such support the Company prospered and in 1927 a series of far-reaching administrative changes began. The Company was renamed East Midland Motor Services Ltd in that year and there was much reorganisation of operations. The same year saw W T Underwood depart.

The vehicles used before the reorganisation had been leased from United, apart from a few purchases (from United and also from acquired operators), but the new Company began to register its own vehicles. The first were still inextricably linked with United, and in fact formed United's G-class. These were fifty Short Brothers-bodied ADC 416A 32-seaters. Thirty second-hand Daimler CBs dating from the early twenties were bought from United. These eighty vehicles all came in 1927. They replaced all other vehicles leased from United. 1928/9 saw a trickle of further second-hand acquisitions and then in 1929 United's M-class of ten AEC Reliances was allocated in its entirety to East Midland. These had United's own Lowestoft-built bodies, which closely resembled those on the contemporary 130-strong United L-class Bristol Bs.

At the turn of the decade East Midland passed into joint LMSR/LNER, and then Tilling, control. E B Hutchinson's control of the Company thus ended. In 1942, when the constituents of British Electric Traction and Tilling went their separate ways, East Midland became a BET company. It passed to the Transport Holding Company in 1963 and on 1st January 1969 to the National Bus Company. There has been further change in the three decades since then, all outside the period covered in Geoffrey Atkins's photographs in this album. It is hoped that an *"East Midland Volume Two"* will be possible in which later matters will be discussed and illustrated.

THE FLEET

In the first half of the 1930s East Midland stayed with AEC for its new purchases, buying ten Regals in 1930, twenty more in 1931, another seven in 1933 and three in 1934. Two Regents arrived in 1932. A Leyland Lion LT5 demonstrator ran in East Midland livery in 1934 (and Geoffrey Atkins was on hand to photograph it). Although no Lions were bought, some Cubs appeared in 1934 and in 1935 the entire year's intake came from Leyland: nineteen TS7 Tigers and six TD4 Titan double-deckers. A fleet-numbering anomaly became evident in 1935. Whereas the single-deckers had been in separate classes (N, L, C and B), the two AEC Regents and the six Titans were all put into the D-class as D1-8. This peculiarity was to persist as long as class letters were used. Thus Leyland Atlanteans in the 1960s were still in the D-class which, in the interim, had included Guys, Daimlers and Crossleys. The Lancashire marque strengthened its hold in the second half of the 1930s. Between 1936 and 1939 ten more Titans and fifty Tigers joined the fleet.

Short Brothers had bodied the 1930 Regals. From then until 1936 bodywork orders went to Brush or Leyland and there was a solitary Burlingham-bodied Tiger TS7 coach in 1936. An innovation in 1937 was an order to Eastern Coach Works for the dual-purpose bodies on that year's thirty TS7s. ECW obtained the 1938 order, too, for the supply of bodies on three TD5 Titans and eleven more TS7s. Five of the new TS8 Tigers in 1938 were also bodied by ECW as were five of the then new Bristol L5G chassis. As if the appearance of ECW-bodied Bristols was not enough, 1939 also saw two Duple-bodied Bedford WTB coaches appear in East Midland livery. Parallel with these purchases in the 'thirties, East Midland had acquired several competing operators, which brought a rich variety of second-hand stock into the fleet. Examples of AJS, Albion, Chevrolet, Citroën, Crossley, Dennis, Dodge, GMC, Guy and Morris, as well as a handful of rather more familiar AECs and Leylands, passed to the Company as a consequence of this activity. All too few of them were given fleet numbers. In many cases they were quickly withdrawn and some were never operated.

The Second World War caused problems in every stratum of the transport industry. Military needs took precedence and public transport operators had a hard time of it. East Midland borrowed nine buses from East Kent in 1940, which helped until the last was returned in mid-1944. New buses were at a premium and were constructed to very basic specification. East Midland was allocated twelve double-deckers from 1941 to 1945: eleven Guy Arabs and a Bristol K5G. Austerity-pattern bodywork came from Strachan, Brush and Roe. Thus the pre-war fleet lasted in service longer than it might have done had there been no war. There was also some rebodying of chassis.

By 1946, the first full year of peace, East Midland was an established BET constituent, and its purchasing policy was not dissimilar from those of others within the group. Leyland and AEC supplied all new chassis up to 1950; Leyland had it all to itself in the next decade; AEC regained a foothold in the 'sixties, as did Bedford. By 1967 Bristol and Eastern Coach Works products had reappeared on the open market, having been closed to non-Tilling group operators since 1948, and East Midland was quick to place an order. The last new AECs appeared in 1968 and thereafter for the period covered by this book Leyland and Bristol had a joint monopoly on East Midland orders. The lion's share of new post-war bodywork in our period came from Leyland, with contributions from Alexander, Burlingham, Duple, Eastern Coach Works, Marshall, MCCW, Plaxton, Saunders Roe, Weymann and Willowbrook. A mixed bag, when compared with the symmetry of the pre-war fleet. The Company carried on its pre-war practice of buying out competing operators, which again brought many second-hand vehicles into the fleet.

In the pages that follow, the photographs are set out with some sense of a year-by-year sequence as vehicles entered the fleet, though this has not been allowed to dogmatically over-rule visual presentation. It is worth stressing again that this book is neither an illustrated history nor a fleet list of East Midland Motor Services Ltd. It is a celebration of some of the riches from the peerless Geoffrey Atkins Collection. What is lacking in vehicles not represented is more than compensated for by the quality of what is.

John Banks
Series Editor
Romiley, Cheshire, August 1999

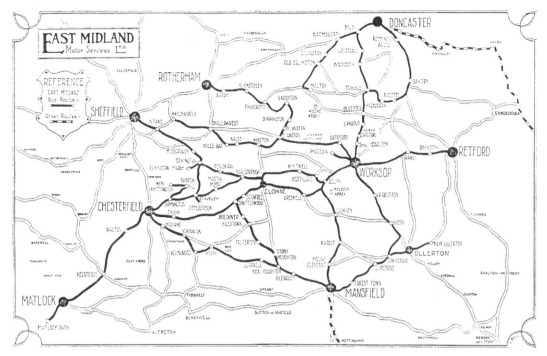

Above: An early route map dated 1st October 1928. The Company's network visibly radiated from Clowne out to Doncaster, Retford, Mansfield, Chesterfield, Sheffield and Rotherham, plus the service 17 spur thrusting south-westward from Chesterfield to Matlock and Matlock Bath. Services south-eastward from Doncaster through Gainsborough, and southward from Mansfield to Nottingham are indicated as "other routes", with no mention of the identity of the operator. In fact the extension from Doncaster was the most westerly of the operations resold to Enterprise & Silver Dawn in June 1927 and the section southward from Mansfield would soon become part of Chesterfield - Mansfield - Nottingham as service 12A.

>> Following page: The area covered by the Company in the mid-fifties - from Doncaster southwards to Nottingham and from Manchester in the West to Retford in the East - in a map based on that used in the June 1957 timetable. East Midland routes are shown in thick grey lines and grey numbers; hatched and plain thin black lines with black numbers show the railway lines and table numbers of the London Midland and Eastern Regions respectively.

Subtle differences between the May 1928 and October 1929 timetables. In 1928 E. B. Hutchinson was still at the helm. The 1929 version was at the beginning of the post-United period, and the line "Late W. T. Underwood, Ltd." had disappeared, as had the "Ltd." after "East Midland".

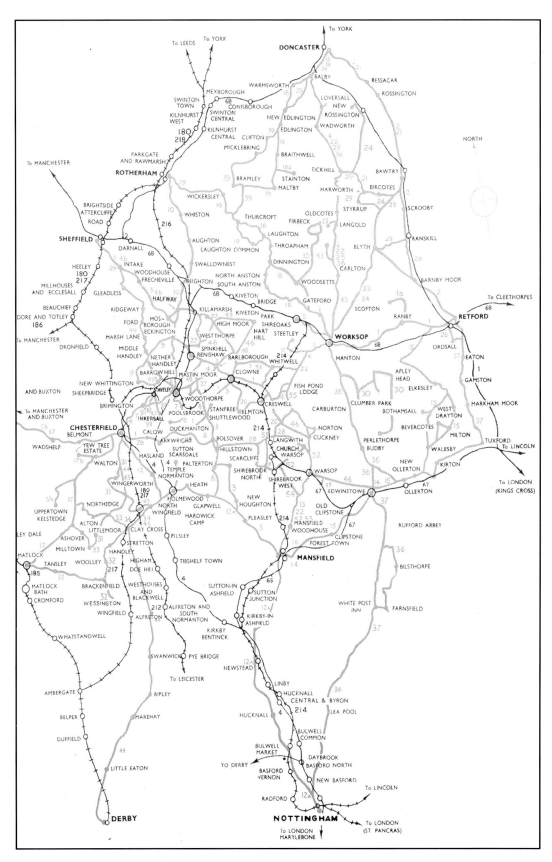

THE UNITED CONNECTION

East Midland was, as we have seen, the W T Underwood operation renamed. Underwood had been in effect a United subsidiary and the latter's influence on the fleet had been profound. United had used an alpha-numeric fleet-numbering system since the early 1920s, in which the letters G and M were allocated to complete batches of buses allocated to East Midland. The 1927 G-class of ADC 416As is represented by **G39** (**RR7439**) *(above)* and the 1929 M-class AEC Reliances by **M4** (**VO739**) *(below)*. The pictures, at Mansfield in November 1934, show the buses in what had been United's livery, though that company had abandoned it in favour of red and white in 1930. M4's route board was a survival from United practice.

THE 1930 AEC REGALS

Above: There were ten of these Regals with Short Brothers coachwork. They took the next class letter after the United-built and supplied AEC Reliances of 1929. The full batch was N1-N10 (VO4071-80). **N4** (**VO4074**) was at Waterdale, Doncaster in September 1933 on a special working.

Below: **N9** (**VO4079**) at the LMS railway station in Mansfield in September 1933. The advertising board on the bus informed the public of the service to Skegness. N9 was on the service to Sheffield. A look at the map shows no reason why Scarcliffe should be singled out for a paper destination label.

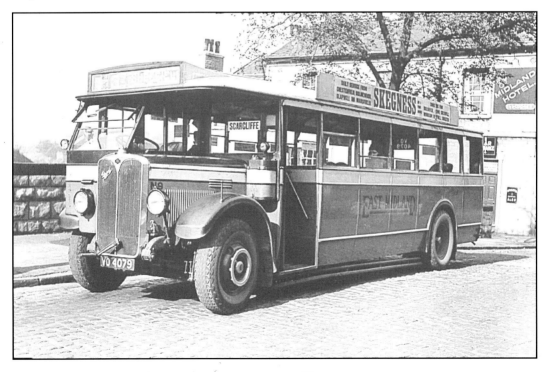

1930 REGALS REBODIED

Bodies of Leyland manufacture were transferred to eight of the 1930 AEC Regals in 1939. The bodies had been supplied in 1935 on Leyland Tiger TS7 chassis. The combination of a chassis and a body from each of the great rival manufacturers of the nineteen-thirties was uncommon, though not unknown. The Leyland bodies were 35-seaters and the Company reused (for the second time) seven of them by transferring them to new AEC Regal chassis in the early post-war period. In these August 1939 pictures at Nottingham, **N8** (**VO4078**) was recently back on the road after the rebodying work. The view below shows the "East Midland" radiator badge made to the same shape as AEC's original.

Above: Inclement weather never put Geoffrey Atkins off if the right bus came along. In this August 1939 view, **N7** (**VO4077**) was splashing through heavy rain in Mansfield Road, Nottingham on the 12A/63 service operated jointly with Trent.

A 1934 DEMONSTRATOR

TJ1139 *(below)* was a diesel-engined Leyland Lion which ran in full East Midland livery on trial in 1934. Few details are known, but its chassis number was 2213 and it had a front-entrance, 32-seat bus body built by Leyland. After its life as a demonstrator was over it went to the fleet of Rees & Williams, Tycroes. It was at Carrington, Nottingham in September 1934.

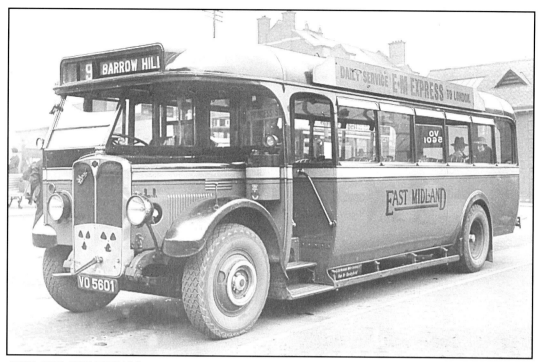

THE 1931 AEC REGALS

For its 1931 Regals East Midland turned to the coachbuilder Brush, of Loughborough. Twenty were supplied, of which the last three were coaches. A new L-class was started by this batch of which the first, **L1 (VO5601)** is seen at Chesterfield in March 1934 *(above)*. The following month produced a masterly portrait *(below)* of **L3 (VO5603)** on the move at Huntingdon Street, Nottingham. By this time roofs were brown. The "white roof effect" on earlier vehicles had been caused by the application of a waterproofing material used when the roof made more of a "corner" with the vertical side panels. Where the roof was one-piece, curling over from horizontal to vertical, the whole lot was painted brown.

Above: The secret of producing after-dark prints such as this one at Huntingdon Street, Nottingham in Ocrober 1936, was known to very few bus photographers. Infinite care in composing the shot, the right type of film and painstaking work in the darkroom combine almost to make it seem possible to walk into the picture and board AEC Regal **L4** (**VO5604**) for the starlit service 36 ride to Doncaster. Two Trent SOSs are beind the Regal.

Below: The Midland Hotel selling Ind Coope's ales is again the September 1933 background at Mansfield LMS railway station, and again an East Midland AEC Regal is waiting to leave for Sheffield. **L13** (**VO5613**) was one of these 1931 Brush bodies to have a shallow dome. Compare with L4 above.

THE 1931 AEC REGAL COACHES

The last three Brush bodies of 1931 were 30 seat coaches for which East Midland's class letters were LC. This pair of pictures of **LC18 (VO5618)** were taken two years apart in exactly the same spot at Huntingdon Street, Nottingham. In the view above, from May 1935, LC18 had its original body and a crest in place of the fleetname transfer, and was on its way from Bradford to London. The later view *(below)*, taken in June 1937, shows LC18 as rebodied with a 1934 Brush bus body which had been converted to coach specification. The coach was employed on the same duty, but was going the other way. The underlined, shaded capitals fleetname transfer reappeared on the replacement body.

THE 1932 AEC REGENTS

East Midland's first new double-deckers came in 1932. A new class was started for D1-2 (VO8001-8002) which were AEC Regents with Brush highbridge bodywork of unusual appearance. The twin front upper-deck windows were fitted at an angle to the front panels. The outside edges were sharply and exaggeratedly swept back. The offside-front view illustrates this oddity well: there is nothing to the right of the central dividing pillar. These Regents were 55-seaters, but could have sat 59 if the upper deck had been built out flush with the between-decks front panels. **D2 (VO8002)** was at Waterdale, Doncaster in April 1934. **G17 (RR7417)** alongside was well-protected against the elements, even in April.

1933/4 - CUBS AND MORE REGALS

Above: The AEC Regal 4 model made its appearance in the fleet in 1933. Brush again built the bodies, which were 32-seaters. They carried on the L-class. **RB7823** was **L23**. It was photographed at Westgate, Mansfield in August 1935. The advertising board extols motor tours to Cleethorpes, Alton Towers, Harrogate as well as a Peak Circular and Evening Tours. *Below:* Five Leyland KP2 Cubs of 1934, forming the C-class, had gone, requisitioned by the military, by 1940. Brand new **C2 (ANN502)** was at Skegness Lawn motor park in July 1934. Appearances by the Leyland Cubs on the long Skegness to Chesterfield service were extremely rare.

Above: Another brand new 1934 vehicle. **L28** (**ANN528**) was in use for private hire work in July 1934. It was parked at Roman Bank, Skegness. Again the roof-board has in-house advertising, this time, appropriately, for private hire. "Radio-coaches" and "sun-saloons" were on offer and the public was exhorted to write in for a quotation. The angle of the photograph reveals the rear registration plate through the back window.

Below: Rather different duties for **L29** (**ANN529**), on service 22 to Doncaster in August 1935 at Westgate, Mansfield. This is the body that was converted to coach specification and exchanged for that on 1931's LC18 *(see page 15, lower).*

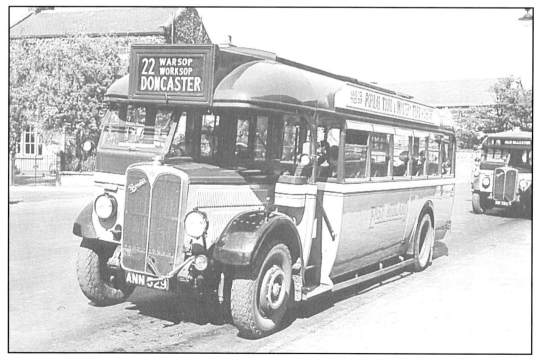

Above: This delightful July 1934 suburban scene in Algitha Road, Skegness reveals some fine three-storey houses, which were destroyed in the second world war. East Midland's **L29 (ANN529)** was setting off on service 25 to Chesterfield. The thoroughfare is devoid of yellow lines, litter, parked cars and other traffic.

Below: East Midland's territory served a widespread coal-mining community. Pit villages often had a brass band which needed conveying to competition and festival venues. East Midland had the regular job of transporting the Creswell Colliery Band. 1934's **LC30 (ANN930)** was converted for this work. A roofrack could be attached for the carriage of instruments and other luggage. This picture was taken from this angle to show the fixing-points on the dome. LC30 was at Huntingdon Street, Nottingham in September 1934.

Above: Nocturnal atmosphere at Huntingdon Street, Nottingham in January 1937. By carefully choosing a wet evening, Geoffrey Atkins turned this picture from a run-of-the-mill (albeit a *quality* mill) shot into a visual masterpiece. It could grace Christmas cards. The offside-front angle of **LC30** (**ANN930**) emphasises the high position of the sidelamps, which were level with the lower edge of the cab windscreen, and that in turn emphasises how shallow the cab windscreen was in relation to the side windows on this Brush design.

THE 1935 LEYLAND TIGERS In 1935 a batch of TS7 Tigers with Brush bodies began Leyland's decades of supremacy in the East Midland fleet. The first ten of the new B-class had Brush bodies, as on **B3** (**BAL603**) seen *(below)* outside Chambers Café at Waterdale, Doncaster in May 1935.

THE 1935 LEYLAND TIGERS

B3's route blind *(<< previous page)* is an interesting one, indicating two separate routes: the 4 from Doncaster to Worksop which connected with the 22 to Mansfield and Chesterfield. A heavily laden bus would go on beyond Worksop, otherwise passengers would be asked to change there.

This page: Leyland succeeded in winning the bodywork order for the rest of the 1935 deliveries. One of each coachbuilder's products are directly compared at Farnsfield in June 1935. Brush-bodied **B10** (**BAL610**) *(above)* and Leyland-bodied **B11** (**BAL611**) *(below)* were going in opposite directions on service 36: buses in both directions entered the village and then reversed to regain the main road.

TIGERS WITH LEYLAND BODIES

The matched pair of Farnsfield pictures on page 21 allows us to consider the possibility that, by 1935, the Brush design was a little dated. The more modern appearance of the Leyland product was almost entirely because of the outswept lower side panels. Brush fought a draw, perhaps, in having a neater destination screen treatment. That on the Leyland body looked like an afterthought. A closer view of the Leyland version is afforded by **B12 (BAL612)** *(above)*, at Doncaster in September 1935, and **B19 (BAL619)** at Nottingham a month earlier *(below)*. Uniquely on B19, the box for the destination screen sloped backwards, more or less following the line of the windscreen, and gave a tidier impression.

TIGERS REBODIED

In late 1949, four of the Brush-bodied 1935 TS7s were rebodied with Willowbrook 35-seat units and renumbered into the N-class. In this form they lasted in the East Midland fleet until 1956/7. In these views of **N2** (**BAL602**, formerly B2) at the Odeon cinema, Nottingham in September 1948 *(above)*, and **N10** (**BAL610**, formerly B10) at the Lawn motor park, Skegness *(below)* in July 1949, the new fleet-numbers are visible, as are the smaller fleetname transfers. B2 retained its polished radiator but had lost the badge, whereas B10 had hung on to its special East Midland badge and had a black painted radiator. The line of these Willowbrook bodies was perhaps spoilt by the prominent roof-mounted ventilators.

THE FIRST LEYLAND TITANS

Leyland saw off the opposition for 1935's double-deckers, too, when it was asked to supply six TD4 Titans fitted with its own 53-seat lowbridge bodies. Leyland had a two-year advantage when its 1934 products were compared with the 1932 Brush-bodied AEC Regents, and the latter were visually very much of an earlier era. Upon learning in May 1935 that the Titans were in service, Geoffrey Atkins hurried to Chesterfield Road, Mansfield to observe them working on the 3 between that town and Sheffield. These two fine photographs resulted. **D4 (BAL704)** was going to Sheffield and **D6 (BAL706)** was running into Mansfield from Sheffield.

TITANS REBODIED

Above: Seven similar lowbridge TD4 Titans were delivered in 1936. One of them, **D14 (BRR914)**, was a fire-damage victim in 1946 and had to be rebodied. Charles Roberts & Company supplied the replacement unit to a semi-utility design in October of that year. The rebodied vehicle was photographed at Westgate, Mansfield in August 1948.

Below: The other six 1936 Titans were rebodied by Willowbrook in 1949. Two ladies sunning themselves on a bench were oblivious of **D15 (BRR915)** behind them at Waterdale, Doncaster in June 1952.

MORE TIGERS FROM LEYLAND AND BRUSH

Fourteen TS7s augmented the B-class in 1936. This time Leyland did not have it all its own way, for five were bodied by Brush and one received a Burlingham coach body. Leyland bodied the remaining eight. Two superlative record shots give us another direct comparison, and again the Leyland design - especially with its improved destination box treatment - had, because of the curved side panels, a more modern aspect than had the Brush. **B26** (**BRR926**), a Leyland-bodied example, was at Westgate, Mansfield (*above*) in May 1936. The Brush version is shown (*below*) on **B28** (**BRR928**) at Huntingdon Street, Nottingham the following September.

THE BRUSH TIGERS UNDER CONSTRUCTION

Above: During a visit to the Brush coach factory in January 1936, Geoffrey Atkins found various units destined for his favourite fleets, including a chassis and at least one body under construction for East Midland. The chassis was number **9247**, which would soon afterwards enter the East Midland fleet as B26, registered BRR932.

Below: At the same time, this body was being finished for East Midland. It is not known for certain whether it went on to the chassis illustrated above, but it is likely that it did.

1937 - EASTERN COACH WORKS BODIES

No fewer than thirty TS7 Tigers came in 1937. They went into a new E-class, which commenced at number 51. Leyland lost the order for bodies for them to Eastern Coach Works at Lowestoft. **E79 (CRR679)** was a March 1937 delivery, photographed at Huntingdon Street, Nottingham the following June. It was working on a joint service with Trent. The announcement to that effect as part of the destination blind was a nice touch, as was the provision of both companies' service numbers: 36 and 64. Other examples of this double numbering appear on pages 12 upper, 29 upper and 36 upper (service 12A/63); 31 upper and 35 upper (service 37/80). These refer to services similarly worked jointly with Trent and in each case the higher number is Trent's. There are many photographs of East Midland buses on the joint services displaying the East Midland service number alone. From a study of the dates it seems probable that, at least for some of the time, both versions were in use concurrently. The introduction of three-track number blinds made double numbering unworkable. As an aside, although we cannot illustrate it, service 44 (Chesterfield - Derby) was jointly operated with Trent and Midland General and in this case the three operators used the same number. Buses of all three are in the photograph at the top of page 35.

LIVERY VARIATIONS AND REBODYING

Above: When delivered, the Eastern Coach Works bodies had the area round the destination screen painted cream. This attractive visual feature contrasted well with the brown roof and window surrounds, but was soon suppressed as shown on page 28. The ECW body had curved side panels; it more than held its own alongside the Leyland design. **E60 ((CRR660)** was at Huntingdon Street, Nottingham in April 1937.

Below: Six of the 1937 E-class Tigers were rebodied by Willowbrook in 1948 and reclassified as Ns. One of them was **N63 (CRR663)**, seen here in June 1952 at Huntingdon Street, Nottingham.

ECW AGAIN IN 1938

Above: The 1937 ECW-bodied TS7 Tigers had been dual-purpose 31-seaters. 1938's eleven TS7s were bodied by ECW as 35-seat service buses. They started an F-class, although the numbers carried on from the previous year's Es. Perhaps the frontal appearance of the bus version was a mild disappointment after the unusual 1937 dual-purpose machines. **F84 (DVO384)** was at Skegness in June 1939.

Below: ECW also bodied three lowbridge, 55-seat Leyland Titan TD5s in 1938. Fourteen-year-old **D16 (DVO316)** was at Chesterfield in March 1952.

THE WARTIME UTILITIES

Above: East Midland took delivery of utility Guy Arabs in each of the years 1942 [2], 1943 [1], 1944 [3] and 1945 [5]. All were lowbridge. The 1942 pair was bodied by Brush and lasted in the fleet until 1954. As always with double-deckers, regardless of chassis make, the Guys were put into the D-class. **D32** (**GAL232**) was at Ollerton Road, Nottingham near Redhill roundabout, in June 1948.

Below: Roe-bodied Guy Arab **D37** (**GNN437**) was one of the 1945 deliveries. It was at Mansfield garage in June 1952. D37 was rebodied in 1954.

THE WARTIME UTILITIES

Above: Another of the 1945 Roe-bodied Guys, **D38 (GNN538)** is seen with its original body at Westgate, Mansfield in May 1951. 1944's **D36 (GNN136)**, also with Roe utility body, was behind, apparently acting as duplicate to D38, which was on service 16 to Forest Town.

Below: The same **D38 (GNN538)** is seen at Mansfield garage in May 1954, soon after its arrival back from Roe, who had rebodied it with a 55-seat lowbridge unit. Several other East Midland wartime Guy Arabs were similarly treated.

REBODIED WARTIME GUY ARABS

Above: **D28** (**GNN328**) was not quite what it might have appeared at first glance. It was a wartime Guy Arab which had been new in 1945 to Baker Brothers, of Warsop. East Midland took this operator over in 1953. GNN328 could neatly be given the fleet number D28 and it was rebodied by Roe in 1953. Another ex-Baker Guy Arab, with original body, is illustrated on page 46. D28 was at Mansfield in May 1954.

Below: East Midland's own **D37** (**GNN437**), which we saw with its original body on page 31, was another Roe rebody. The photograph was taken at Mansfield garage in May 1954.

1946 - REAPPEARANCE OF THE AEC REGAL

Above: The A-class AEC Regals with Weymann 35-seat bodies of 1946 were the first buses built to post-war peacetime standards to enter the fleet. They were very similar to some London Transport T-types. There were ten of them and our illustrations are of the first and last of the batch. **A1 (GRR301)** was at Huntingdon Street, Nottingham in May 1947.

Below: **A10 (GRR310)** was being washed by garage staff at Mansfield in February 1955. The oblong registration plate below the radiator had given way to a square plate on the dash.

THE FIRST POST-WAR DOUBLE-DECKERS

Above: Two all-Leyland Titan PD1 53-seaters came in 1947. In this Huntingdon Street, Nottingham view in early 1948, the second of them, **D43 (HNN143)** was flanked by two of the 1948 Leyland Titan PD2/1s. On the left was **D61 (HVO861)** and on the right **D51 (HVO851)**. The difference in front panel and mudguard treatment between the two types is clearly shown. *Below:* The same bus at Mansfield garage in May 1956. This is our first illustration (although not the first photograph Geoffrey Atkins took) of the new red and ivory livery introduced in 1955. Apart from the change of colour, the livery was much simplified, with but one lighter band to relieve the monotony.

1948 TITANS

Above: Another fine after-dark view at Huntingdon Street, Nottingham. In April 1948, Leyland Titan PD2/1 **D63** (**HVO863**), then just two months old, was awaiting its departure time on the joint-with-Trent service to Chesterfield.

Below: The red livery with single ivory band is carried by one of the PD2/1s. **D59** (**HVO859**) was at Clowne garage in January 1956. Clowne garage dated from Underwood days. It had been the Company's first and came into use in the early nineteen-twenties.

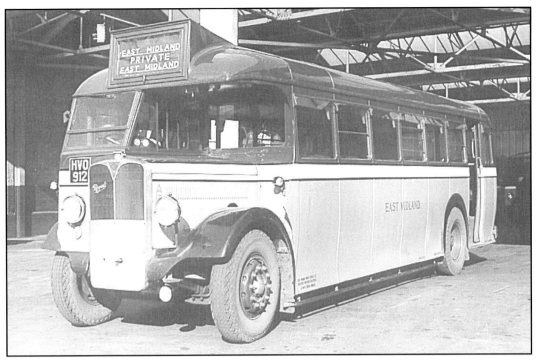

OUT-OF-THE-ORDINARY REGALS

Above: Additions to the A-class in 1947 and 1948 were on the AEC Regal III chassis, fourteen of them, which were fitted with second-hand Leyland bodies dating from the mid-nineteen-thirties. They had originally been carried by Leyland Tigers, then by pre-war AEC Regals. The 1948 chassis were their third, therefore. Representative is **A12** (**HVO912**), seen at Mansfield garage in March 1948.

Below: **AC2** (**HVO902**) was one of a pair of 1948 Windover-bodied AEC Regal III coaches which were withdrawn after less than ten years in service. AC2 was at Huntingdon Street, Nottingham in August 1950.

NEW BODIES FOR OLD

Above: The 1947/48 AEC Regals which, when new, had had pre-war Leyland bodies, were equipped with new Willowbrook units in 1952. In the same year they were renumbered into the K-class. **K11** (**HVO911**), of 1947, was dealt with in January 1952. A few weeks later, in March, it was at Chesterfield on service 17 to Matlock Bath. In 1999 service number 17 is a rare survivor from the original 1920s operations.

Below: 1948's Willowbrook-rebodied **K22** (**HVO922**), at Chesterfield on the same occasion, was waiting to leave on service 9 to Eckington.

1949 - MORE WEYMANN AEC REGALS

The Weymann 35-seat single-deck body was specified for some AEC Regal IIIs to be delivered in 1949. The fleet numbers carried on from 1948's A-class Regal IIIs, but the type letter was changed to H. The well-balanced, clean lines of the 1946 Weymann bodies seemed somewhat compromised on this version of three years later because of the larger, rather cumbersome destination screen box. **H31** (**KAL131**) *(above)* was on private hire work at Union Road, Nottingham in August 1949; **H35** (**KAL135**) *(below)* was working service 18 to Dinnington at Glasgow Paddocks, Doncaster in July 1949. Both buses had entered service the previous June and thus were brand new in these pictures.

SECOND-HAND TIGERS

In the late nineteen-forties East Midland had some Roe-bodied Leyland Tiger TS7s on loan from the Yorkshire Woollen District Transport Company, of Dewsbury. Ten of them were purchased early in 1949 and sent to Willowbrook for rebodying. **N102 (HD5617)**, at Huntingdon Street, Nottingham in May 1951 *(above)*, was in the standard livery. Its radiator was painted black and had a "Leyland" badge. **N103 (HD5803)**, at the same location in August 1955 *(below)*, differed in some details. It had no cream waistband, which gave a slightly drab effect. On the other hand, its polished radiator was equipped with a cast "East Midland" badge.

1950 LEYLAND TITANS

No fewer than twenty PD2/1 Leylands came in 1950/1. They would be the last Titans until 1955. By then Leyland would have ceased building bodywork and MCCW bodies would be ordered. These views of the last batch of all-Leyland East Midland Titans are of **D70** (**KRR70**) at Huntingdon Street, Nottingham in April 1950 *(above)*, and of **D77** (**KRR77**) *(below)* at Clowne garage in May 1954. From these Titans onwards, a revised destination blind layout, similar to that featured on the Roe-rebodied Guy Arabs, was specified. D70, a March 1950 delivery, had an upper-deck cream band, a feature omitted on D77, which entered the fleet two months later. The side destination blind is a fine period touch.

AN AUSTERE LIVERY AND MORE REGALS

Above: Another example of the modified, less attractive, East Midland livery seen in the mid-1950s. The all-over shade was a sandy-coloured brown, with only the upstairs window frames and roof in the old dark brown. The loss of the cream relief made a difference out of all proportion to its size. **D85 (KRR85),** an all-Leyland PD2/1 of 1951 was at Huntingdon Street, Nottingham in March 1956. *Below:* For the bodywork on its 1950 batch of AEC Regal IIIs East Midland returned to Willowbrook. Fleet-number practice saw another change, too; the class letter became J and the numbers carried on from 1949's H38, but with 200 added. Thus **KVO243,** at Glasgow Paddocks, Doncaster in May 1953, was **J243.**

ACQUISITIONS AND UNDERFLOOR ENGINES

Above: Representative of the many second-hand vehicles which entered the East Midland fleet as a consequence of the buying out of other operators was **AC3** (**LAL358**), a 1950 AEC Regal III with Burlingham coach body acquired with the fleet of Portland Coachways, of Worksop, in June 1951.

Below: East Midland plunged into the operation of underfloor-engined vehicles in 1952 with no fewer than twenty Leyland-bodied Royal Tigers. The R-series of numbers, commencing at 301, was begun for them. The traditional livery sat well on brand new **R309** (**MRR309**) at Huntingdon Street in April 1952.

LIVERY VARIATIONS FOR THE 1952 LEYLAND ROYAL TIGERS

R303 (**MRR303**) was two years old at Chesterfield *(above)* in April 1954. It had the simplified paint scheme which lacked the cream band, and had lost its wheelnut ring guard. We have seen the red livery on earlier pages: the photograph below was the first of it taken by Geoffrey Atkins. Critical comment about the loss of traditional liveries grows stale and repetitious, but time has not lessened the disappointment many of us felt when the old colours, which had linked East Midland so colourfully to its birth in the 1920s, disappeared. The shock was the more keenly felt over examples which had little or no relief from all-over dark red, such as **R319** (**MRR319**) at Wellington Circus, Nottingham in September 1955.

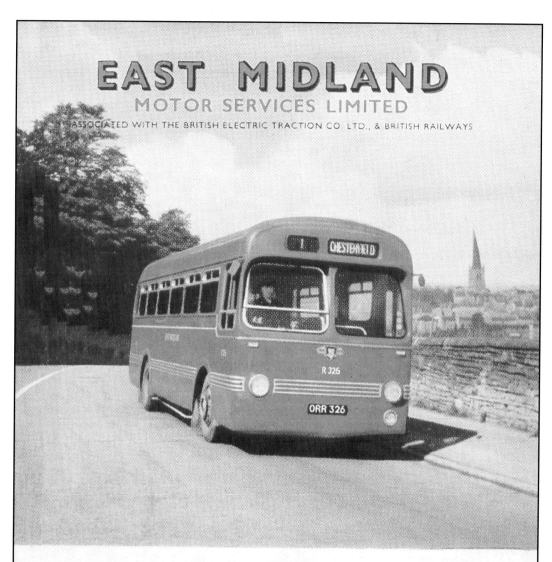

EAST MIDLAND
MOTOR SERVICES LIMITED
IN ASSOCIATED WITH THE BRITISH ELECTRIC TRACTION CO LTD., & BRITISH RAILWAYS

9th
JUNE
1957

OFFICIAL
TIME TABLE
UNTIL FURTHER NOTICE

PRICE
6D

THE BAKER BROTHERS ACQUISITION

On 1st March 1953 the vehicles of Baker Brothers, of Warsop, were absorbed into the East Midland fleet. The heterogeneous collection of buses and coaches included nine double-deckers, of which Geoffrey Atkins recorded five. **D91 (EML154)** *(above)* was a 1936 former AEC Regent demonstrator with Park Royal 56-seat highbridge bodywork. It was at Mansfield garage in May 1953 and still carried the Baker livery. **D29 (GAL832)**, at the same place and date *(below)*, had been rebuilt and repainted by its new owner. It was a 1944 Massey-bodied Guy Arab utility. Another ex-Baker Brothers Guy Arab, rebodied by Roe, is illustrated on page 33. D91 was quickly withdrawn later in 1953, but D29 lasted into 1957.

EX-BAKER BROTHERS DAIMLERS

Above: **D92** (**GRR919**) was a Massey bodied highbridge Daimler CWD6. The downward-swooping beading on both decks was ignored, when East Midland repainted the bus, in favour of a continuation of the lined cream bands. The photograph was taken at Mansfield garage in May 1953.

Below: Another Daimler, this time with Charles Roberts & Company highbridge bodywork, was photographed at Mansfield in August 1955. **D93** (**KNN715**) was a 1949 CVD6. These Daimlers were withdrawn in 1956 and 1958. All the ex-Baker Brothers vehicles had gone by the end of 1960.

A CROSSLEY DOUBLE-DECKER

East Midland took three Crossleys from Baker Brothers. Two were double-deckers and Geoffrey Atkins photographed one of them twice, in different liveries. **D94 (JAL363)** was a Crossley-bodied DD42/7 which had been new in 1949 as a highbridge 56-seater. It was one of the longest-lived ex-Baker Brothers vehicles, lasting into 1960. In the first picture *(above)*, taken at Mansfield in May 1953, D94 was still in Baker Brothers livery, with East Midland fleetname and fleet-number transfers. In the view below, taken in August 1955, the Crossley was in exactly the same spot, almost to the inch, and had been repainted into East Midland colours.

MORE UNDERFLOOR ENGINES

The Royal Tiger had been found heavy and over-engineered for the domestic market. The Tiger Cub was a lighter-weight solution to the problem and East Midland took thirty-one in 1954/55. The bus version, of which there were 25, was bodied as a 44-seater by Saunders-Roe (Saro). **R324** (**ORR324**), in original livery *(above)*, was at Chesterfield in April 1954, one month after entering service. Six coaches on the Tiger Cub chassis had Burlingham Seagull bodies with 41 seats and centre entrances. A lowering sky at Skegness Lawn car park in July 1954 *(below)* throws **C22** (**PVO622**) almost into three-dimensional relief. The underlined fleetname seemed to be a compromise between the older and newer styles.

TIGER CUB LIVERY VARIATIONS

Above: **R343** (**ORR343**), at Huntingdon Street, Nottingham in July 1960, had the drab all-red livery with no relieving lighter colours. This is another service 37 to Retford picture.

Below: An amended livery incorporating white window surrounds was a vast improvement. Just how much it enhanced a vehicle's appearance is demonstrated by Tiger Cub **R341** (**ORR341**) at Chesterfield in May 1964.

1955 - THE ORION TITANS

The face of the East Midland double-decker changed radically once Leyland bodywork became unavailable. The year's PD2/20 Leyland Titans had MCCW Orion bodies with what were appositely called "tin fronts" in a style which had been developed for Midland Red. **D105 (RRR105)** and **D100 (RRR100)** at Sherwood, Nottingham in July 1955 *(above)* highlight the practice East Midland had of sending out simultaneous service 37 (to Retford) and 36 (to Doncaster) departures from Huntingdon Street. The fully fronted Titans suffered from brake overheating problems. Air intakes were inserted into the panels below the headlights. 1956's **D107 (UNN107)**, in red livery, demonstrates in August 1958.

1956 LEYLAND TIGER CUBS

Above: Dual-purpose 41-seat bodywork in reversed livery from Willowbrook was specified for eight Tiger Cubs in 1956. **C34 (TVO234)** was at Wellington Circus, Nottingham in March 1957. There was a different transfer for the offside *(see page 55)* so that the fleetname leaned forwards on both sides.

Below: Tiger Cub service buses in 1956 were 44-seaters with MCCW bodies. In this 1964 shot at Mansfield garage, **R355 (URR355)** had graduated to the less harsh livery of dark red with white window surrounds.

TIGER CUB LIVERY VARIATIONS IN UNUSUAL LOCATIONS

Above: **R350** (**URR350**) in a version of the all-over red livery, with minimal relief given by the thin strip of beading underneath the windows. The fleetname was contained in a distorted rectangle which sat ill with the functional, upright lines of the MCCW body. It was at Lower Mosley Street coach station, Manchester in May 1960.

Below: In what was effectively a reversed livery (the beading below the windows was dark red), **R353** (**URR353**) was at Bridlington railway station in August 1957. **C30** (**TVO230**) was alongside.

PROGRESS WITH UNDERFLOOR-ENGINED DESIGNS

Above: **R365** (**WNN365**) was a 1958 Leyland Tiger Cub with Weymann 44-seat bodywork. Even when clean and shiny and with a light-coloured beading strip the red livery could not shake off its gloomy appearance. R365 was at Huntingdon Street, Nottingham in June 1962.

Below: Reversed liveries for dual-purpose vehicles leavened the pervading red in the early nineteen-sixties. This one, carried by 1960's Weymann-bodied AEC Reliance **C255** (**255ENN**) at Huntingdon Street in September 1963, had a peculiar descender underneath the AEC badge, apparently to mask an air intake.

BEDFORDS AND BURLINGHAMS

A most attractive combination appeared in 1961 with three Burlingham-bodied coaches on Leyland Leopard L2 chassis *(above)*. The livery was a half-and-half dark red and ivory, happily proportioned, which suited the coachwork (which *just* escaped the charge of being "flamboyant") well. Note that the *offside* fleetname script leans forward (see page 52). **C258 (258GRR)** is illustrated at Mansfield Market Place in May 1963. Almost as striking were three Duple-bodied Bedford VAMs of 1966. This time the livery was a triple-deck sandwich with three areas each of red and ivory, and yet another style of fleetname. **C280 (FNN280D)**, at Llandudno in July 1966 *(below)*, had been in service since May.

LONGER CHASSIS AND YET MORE LIVERY VARIATIONS

Above: Thirty-six-feet-long chassis began to appear in the fleet in 1963. Among 1963's substantial intake was a pair of Alexander-bodied Leyland PSU3/3R Leopard 49-seaters for express work. The light and dark portions of the livery were well-balanced and suited the elegant, uncluttered coachwork. **C267** (**267PRR**) was at Huntingdon Street, Nottingham in October 1964 waiting to cruise down to London.

Below: An exact contemporary of C267 was **L407** (**407RRR**), another Leyland Leopard, this time bodied as a 53-seat bus by Willowbrook and later repainted red. It was at Mansfield garage in September 1963.

Above: A Willowbrook-bodied Leyland Leopard 53-seater of 1963 which was red from new. This is an October 1968 shot at Huntingdon Street, Nottingham of **L403** (**403RRR**).

THE REAR-ENGINED REVOLUTION BEGINS

Below: An early customer for the Leyland Atlantean, East Midland placed ten in service in each of 1959 and 1960 and another twelve in 1961. Weymann 73-seat (72 in 1961) bodywork was fitted on which a substantial cream band split the red livery into two halves. One of the 1959 examples, **D134** (**134BRR**), was at Westgate, Mansfield in May 1960. Across the road was one of the 1960 batch, **D144** (**144ENN**).

DEMONSTRATORS

Above: East Midland tried out **525LMJ**, a Duple-bodied Bedford VAL, in 1964. In this April view it was at Huntingdon Street, Nottingham. No orders for Bedford VALs resulted.

Below: The Guy Wulfrunian, **8072DA**, which was in East Midland service briefly in 1960, similarly failed to impress enough for orders to be placed. Whatever its mechanical difficulties, the Wulfrunian was undeniably a purposeful machine in appearance. The livery was rather plain but a nice touch was the Indian's head crest and the name "Guy Wulfrunian" on the sides. It was at Sheffield in September 1960.

DOUBLE-DECK VARIETY

Above: The Weymann version of the Orion body, as carried by 1957's **D124 (WAL124)**, a Leyland Titan PD3/4 with exposed radiator. The Orion was clean and functional, let down only by the small side windows seemingly lost in acres of drab red. This is a July 1957 scene at Huntingdon Street, Nottingham.

Below: East Midland inherited a trio of Cravens-bodied ex-London Transport RTs when it took over the fleet of Wass Brothers Ltd, of Mansfield, in 1958. **D45 (JXC219)** was at Mansfield in July 1959. It was originally London Transport RT1456. The East Midland Cravens RTs ran only until 1960.

ALBION LOWLANDERS

As owners of thirty-two 1959-61 Leyland Atlanteans, East Midland might have been expected to augment that total. The next double-deckers, on the contrary, were Albion Lowlanders. Examples bodied by Alexander and MCCW were delivered in the period 1962-66. The Atlantean made a confident come-back between 1965 and 1971 until again being eclipsed, this time more comprehensively, by the Bristol VRT. One each of the Albion Lowlanders is illustrated. **D169** (**169NVO**), with Alexander body *(above)*, was at Mansfield garage in September 1966; **D183** (**GNN183D**) was an MCCW version, seen at Huntingdon Street, Nottingham in July 1967 *(below)*. All East Midland Lowlanders had Albion radiator badges.

MORE LEYLAND ATLANTEANS

Above: East Midland stayed with Alexander for bodywork when again ordering Leyland Atlanteans in the second half of the nineteen-sixties. **D193 (PNN193F)** was a 1968 example, photographed in July 1972 at Mansfield depot. An MCCW-bodied Albion Lowlander (**D186**) was on the other side of the road.

Below: Standing in more-or-less the same spot under a year earlier, in September 1971, one of East Midland's last batch of new Atlanteans waits to depart for Clowne. **D197 (CRR197J)** had entered service the previous July.

BRISTOL AND EASTERN COACH WORKS

Above : East Midland was prompt to place orders for Bristol chassis carrying Eastern Coach Works bodies as soon as they were available on the open market. The first (RELL service buses) entered service in 1967. The first VRT double-deckers appeared in 1971, the same year as the last Alexander-bodied Atlanteans. **D103 (HAL103K)** was less than six months old when caught at Mansfield depot in March 1972.

Below: **C292 (EVO292J)**, also new in 1971, was a dual-purpose 49-seater bus-outline body on an RELH chassis for express work. In this June 1971 Nottingham view it was about to leave for Sheffield.

BRISTOL SERVICE BUSES

Above: The new, open-market situation permitted operators to specify other than Eastern Coach Works bodies on Bristol chassis. In 1969 East Midland took some Leyland-engined LHs with 45-seat Willowbrook bodies. **O528 (UNN528G)** was one, seen at Huntingdon Street, Nottingham in June 1969.

Below: The 36 service to Doncaster was graced by a dual-door Bristol RELL6G Eastern Coach Works 44-seater in August 1971. **O544 (FNN544J)** was just over two months old when this picture was taken in Huntingdon Street, Nottingham. FNN544J was withdrawn in 1982.

EAST MIDLAND

PRIVATE HIRE

For your next Party Outing consult our
Private Hire Department

QUOTATIONS GLADLY GIVEN —WITHOUT OBLIGATION

Your Pleasure is our Business

PARCELS

- We convey parcels at moderate charges between all the principal towns and villages served by the Company.

See page xxv for scale of charges.